WHY DO WE CEL HALLOWEEN?

Holidays Kids Book
Children's Holiday Books

BABY PROFESSOR

EDUCATION KIDS

Speedy Publishing LLC

40 E. Main St. #1156

Newark, DE 19711

www.speedypublishing.com

Copyright 2017

Halloween is a fun holiday, a bright event at the end of October, as the nights get longer and we head into winter. But what is Halloween all about? Let's take a look.

WHAT HAPPENS AT HALLOWEEN

In North America and other parts of the world, children and some adults put on costumes and go to visit houses nearby. They shout "trick or treat!" and the homeowner offers them candy or other treats.

How did this tradition get started, and why do people do what they do?

BOYS IN HALLOWEEN COSTUMES TRICK OR TREATING

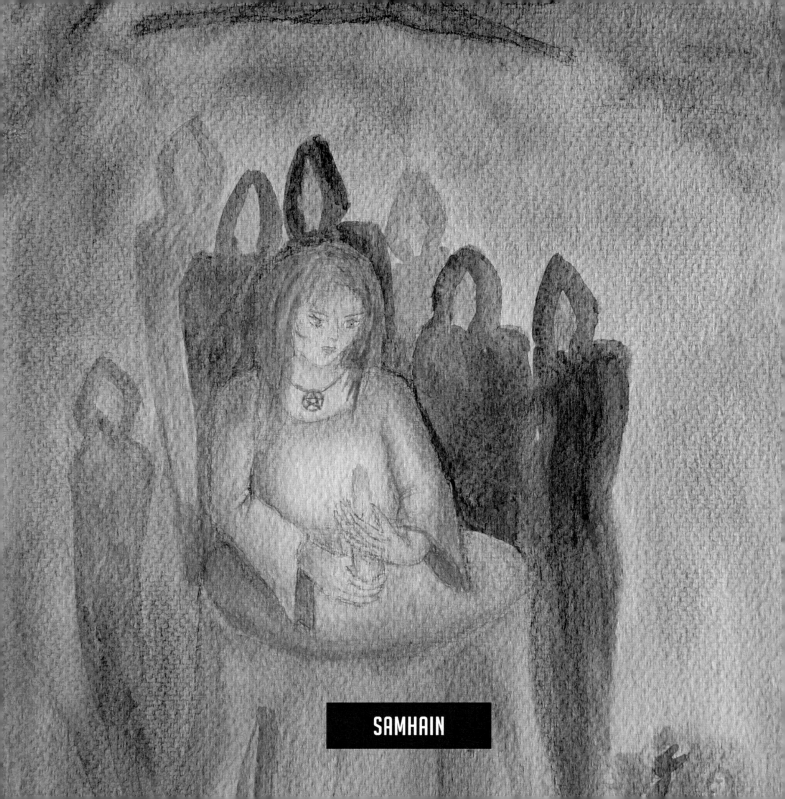

SAMHAIN

THE HISTORY OF HALLOWEEN

The origins of Halloween are in a religious festival, Samhain, that the Celtic people in northern Europe celebrated at least two thousand years ago. Samhain was observed in what is now Ireland, northern France, and the United Kingdom, and marked the start of the Celtic new year on November 1.

November 1, for the Celts, was the end of harvest time and the start of winter. The days grew shorter and the weather grew colder, and for people living in a time without electric lights or heat, it was an uneasy part of the year. You had to rely on the food and fuel you had stored during the summer and autumn, and there was less you could do outdoors. The extra hours of darkness meant there were more hours when things could sneak up on you!

The Celts believed that there was a world of the living and a world of the dead. On the night when the old year ended and the new year began, the barrier between those two worlds opened for a while. Spirits of the dead could move among the living, and if they were not careful the living could find themselves in the world of the dead.

The spirits that came into the world of the living could cause trouble, scaring people and destroying buildings and crops. But they could also bring news of what was to happen in the new year. Finding out what was coming was as important to the Celts then as it is to us now.

BONFIRE

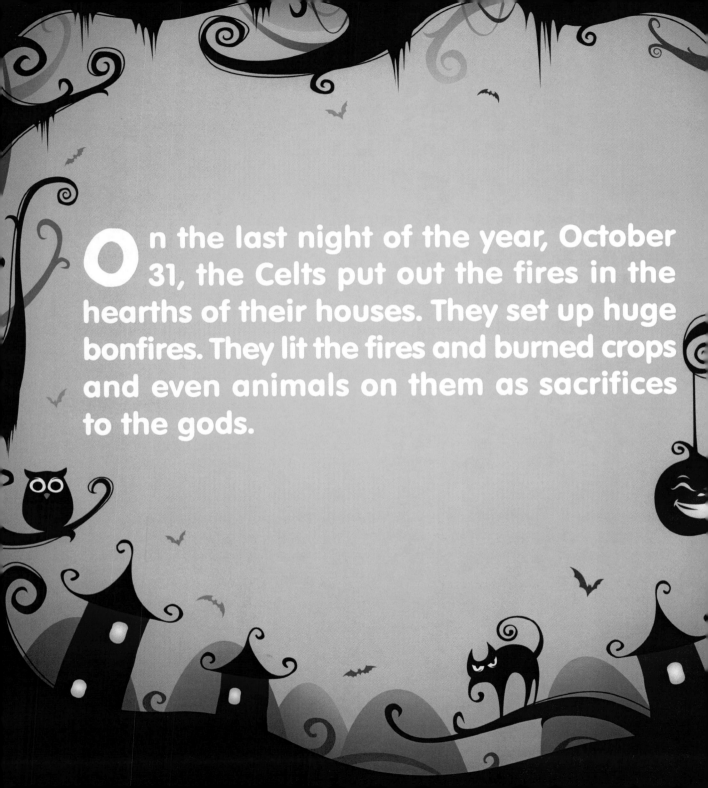

On the last night of the year, October 31, the Celts put out the fires in the hearths of their houses. They set up huge bonfires. They lit the fires and burned crops and even animals on them as sacrifices to the gods.

Some of the Celts, especially the priests, wore animal heads and skins, danced around the fires and tried to predict the future. At the end of the evening, people took fire from the bonfires and lit the fires in their hearths again, to start the new year with new light and hoping for the blessing of their gods.

CELTIC AND ROMAN FESTIVALS MERGE

The Roman Empire conquered most Celtic territory by the first century CE. England was part of the Roman Empire for about four hundred years, and France for even longer. During that time, the Celtic festival Samhain was joined with two Roman festivals.

LONDON ENGLAND

STATUE OF POMONA

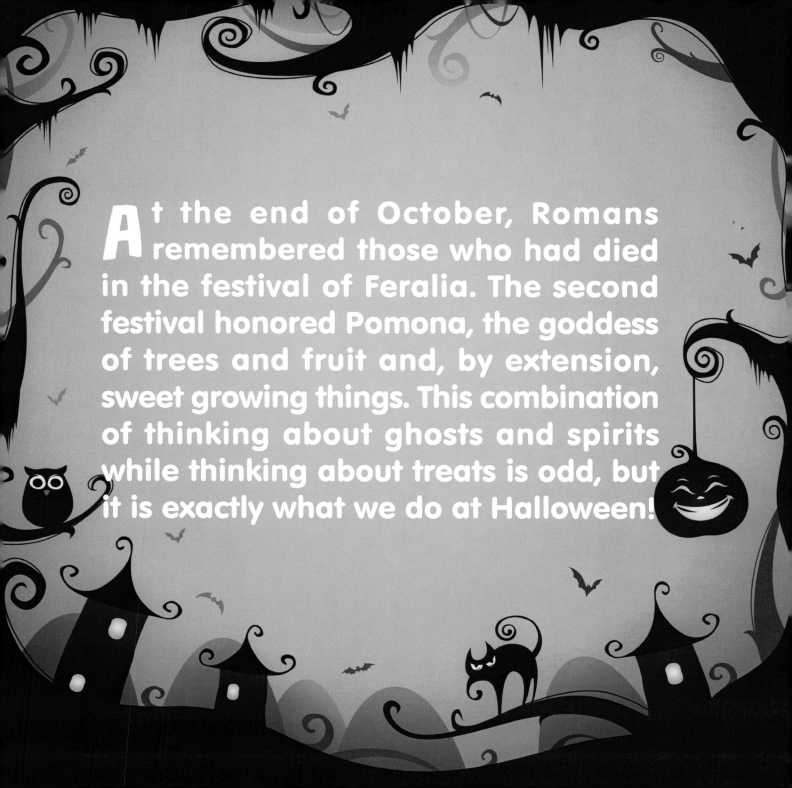

At the end of October, Romans remembered those who had died in the festival of Feralia. The second festival honored Pomona, the goddess of trees and fruit and, by extension, sweet growing things. This combination of thinking about ghosts and spirits while thinking about treats is odd, but it is exactly what we do at Halloween!

ADDING A CHRISTIAN FESTIVAL

In 609 CE, the Christian church established a festival to honor martyrs. Christian martyrs were people who had been killed because they believed in Jesus Christ and followed him as their Lord even if the government said it was illegal.

THE ROMAN FORUM IN ROME, ITALY.

There had been thousands of Christian martyrs between the time of Christ and when Christianity became an approved religion in the Roman Empire, in the fourth century CE. Thousands more lost their lives for their faith when taking the Christian message to people outside the empire.

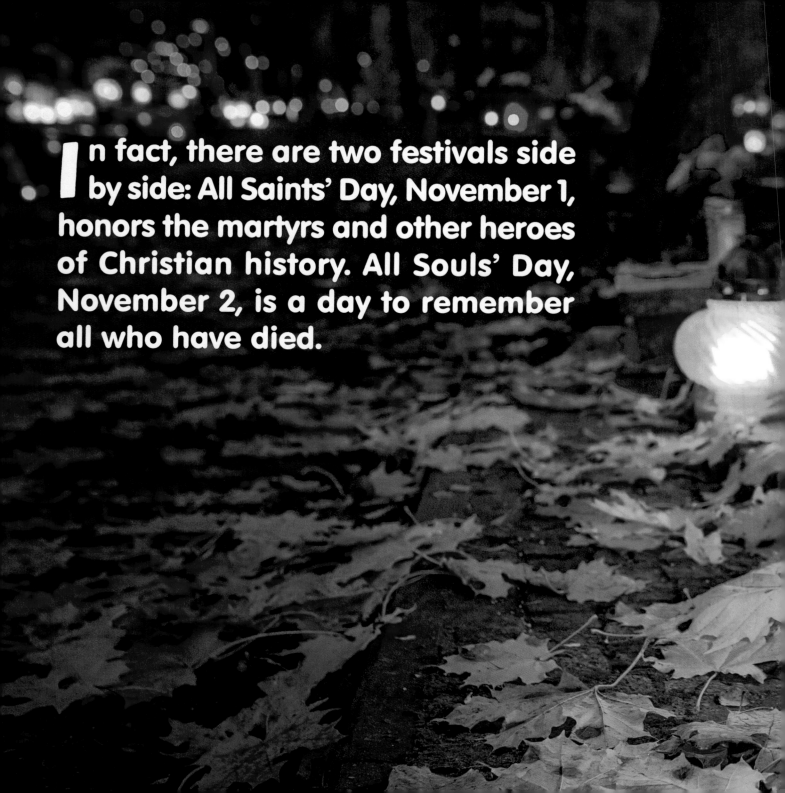

In fact, there are two festivals side by side: All Saints' Day, November 1, honors the martyrs and other heroes of Christian history. All Souls' Day, November 2, is a day to remember all who have died.

COLORFUL CANDLES AT THE CEMETERY ON ALL SAINTS DAY

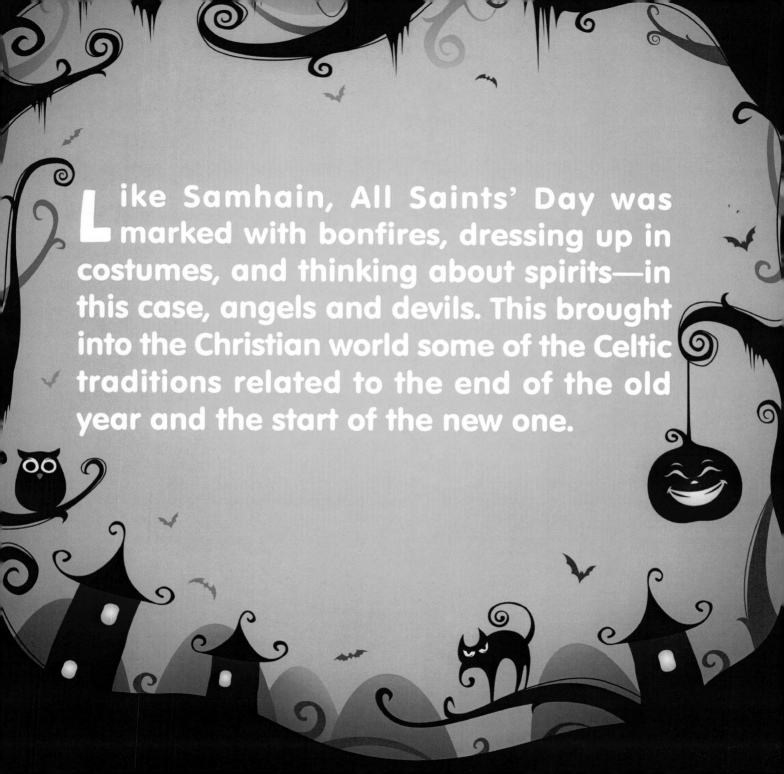

Like Samhain, All Saints' Day was marked with bonfires, dressing up in costumes, and thinking about spirits—in this case, angels and devils. This brought into the Christian world some of the Celtic traditions related to the end of the old year and the start of the new one.

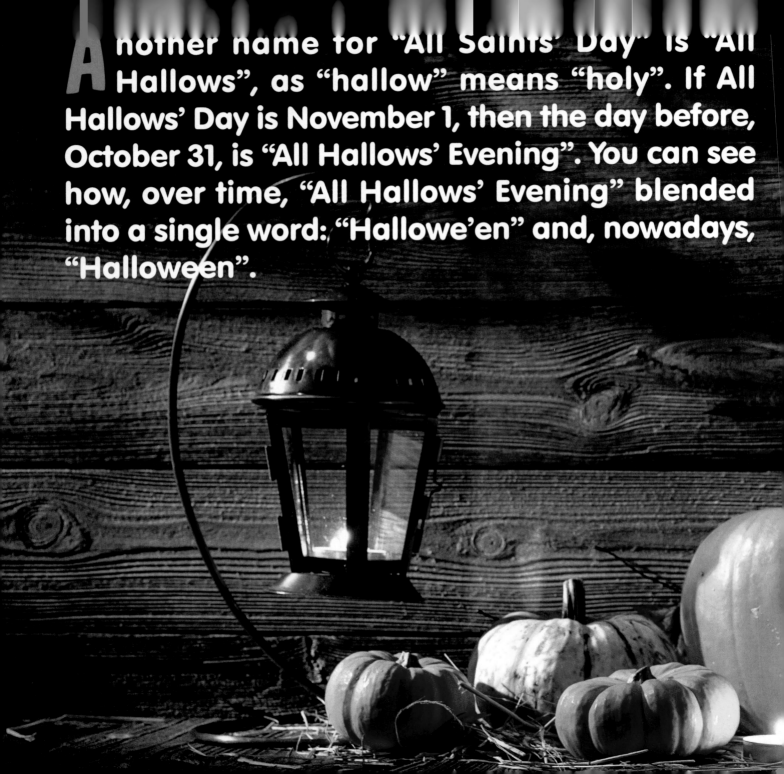

Another name for "All Saints' Day" is "All Hallows", as "hallow" means "holy". If All Hallows' Day is November 1, then the day before, October 31, is "All Hallows' Evening". You can see how, over time, "All Hallows' Evening" blended into a single word: "Hallowe'en" and, nowadays, "Halloween".

TRICKS OR TREATS

When we shout, "Trick or treat!" at a door on Halloween, what are we doing? We are carrying on two ancient traditions, joined together.

LITTLE GIRL TRICK-OR-TREATING ON HALLOWEEN

TRICK

In Medieval Europe there were long-standing traditions of the "feast of fools", a day when servants were the masters and people could do all sorts of wild things without getting in trouble. The idea was that if people could cut loose for one day in the year, perhaps they would behave better the rest of the year!

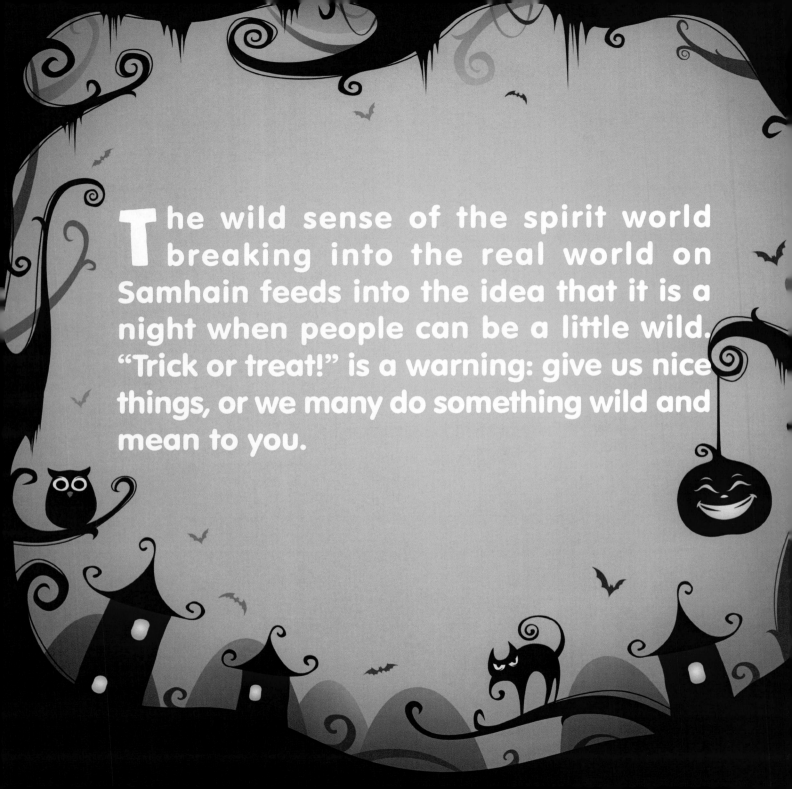

The wild sense of the spirit world breaking into the real world on Samhain feeds into the idea that it is a night when people can be a little wild. "Trick or treat!" is a warning: give us nice things, or we many do something wild and mean to you.

KIND LITTLE CHILD GIVES APPLE TO A HOMELESS PERSON

TREAT

In the All Souls' Day parades in England, poor people would stand by the parade route or go from house to house. Homeowners, or people in the parade, would give them gifts of food. One of the main gifts was "soul cakes", or pastries. The poor person would get some food in return for praying for the dead relatives of the person who made the gift.

This practice was called "going a-souling", and is what lies behind our going from door to door, looking for treats, on October 31.

HALLOWEEN IN NORTH AMERICA

When the Puritans started colonies in New England in the 17th century, they tried to avoid old practices that they felt were useless superstitions. They did not even celebrate Christmas, so you can imagine what they thought of Halloween!

Halloween first came into practice in North America in Maryland and the southern colonies. The traditions mixed with Native American customs, so the early Halloween events were "play parties" when people got together to celebrate a good harvest and tell stories of their ancestors. A lot of those stories had elements of ghost stories, with the ghosts of past people coming back to scare or play tricks on people now. People would play tricks on their neighbors, and blame them on the Halloween ghosts!

YOUNG IRISH GIRL

THE IRISH ARRIVE

In the later part of the nineteenth century, many Irish people moved to the United States because there was a famine in Ireland. They brought with them many traditions, including dressing up in costumes and going from door to door to ask for treats.

A SECULAR HOLIDAY

Many people in the United States were troubled by the emphasis on ghosts and demons. There was a move to change Halloween into more of a community celebration: more fun, fewer phantoms!

By the 1930s, Halloween featured parties, games, and parades more than it did witches and ghosts. Communities made efforts to cut down on the "trick" part and build up the "treat" part of the holiday.

SPOOKY ORANGE HALLOWEEN CANDIES

HALLOWEEN FUN FACTS

Here are some neat things to know abo[ut] Halloween:

- Of all the candy sold every year in t[he] United States, 25 percent is boug[ht] to give away on Halloween.

In the eighteenth century, young women believed they could learn about their future husband on Halloween, by doing certain tricks. They would stand in front of a mirror in a dark room and try to make out their future husband's face behind them in the shadowy reflection.

APPLE PEEL

Or they would take apple peels and throw them over their shoulder, then turn around and see if the peels formed letters: the letters could be the initials of the name of the man they would marry!

- Dressing in costume for Halloween goes back thousands of years. In part, it is an attempt to confuse any ghosts who might be nearby, and in part it lets people see if they can scare or startle their neighbors without the neighbor knowing who played the trick on them.

EVIL WITCH HOLDING HER CRYSTAL BALL

IRISH COLCANNON POTATO AND CABBAGE MASH

- People used to put food outside their homes for passing ghosts, so the ghosts would not try to enter the house.

- In Ireland the Halloween meal might have mashed potatoes. Among the potatoes would be a ring. Whoever found the ring was assured of romance in the coming year!

In Scotland, a young woman would take a handful of hazelnuts and throw them in the fire one by one. She would give each one the name of a young man she might like to marry. The nut that burned down to ashes instead of exploding or popping would indicate the man she would marry.

LIFE IS FULL OF CELEBRATIONS

All around the world people have celebrations to mark special days, to remember great events, or to celebrate things like birthdays and weddings.

Learn more about world holidays in Baby Professor books like The Snowman's Got Frostbite! - Winter Around the World, The Chinese Festivals, and Women-Centered Holidays from Around the World.

Made in United States
North Haven, CT
01 October 2023

42214747R00038